Rosa Parks

Maryann N. Weidt

HAMPTON-BROWN

THE EXCHANGE

Can we fight without violence? How?

To Sue, with love and admiration

Illustrations by Tim Parlin.

Rosa Parks by Maryann N. Weidt. Text copyright © 2003 by Maryann N. Weidt. Illustrations copyright © 2003 by Lerner Publications Company. This edition is published by Hampton-Brown, by arrangement with Lerner Publications Company, a division of Lerner Publishing Group, 241 First Avenue North, Minneapolis, MN 55401 U.S.A.

On-Page Coach ™ (introductions, questions, on-page glossaries), The Exchange, back cover summary © Hampton-Brown.

Hampton-Brown
P.O. Box 223220
Carmel, California 93922
800-333-3510
www.hampton-brown.com

Printed in the United States of America

ISBN-13: 978-0-7362-2777-3
ISBN-10: 0-7362-2777-6

08 09 10 11 12 13 14 10 9 8 7 6 5

TABLE OF CONTENTS

INTRODUCTION   5

1. A HARD CHILDHOOD   6

2. UNFAIR RULES   15

3. ROSA SAYS NO   22

4. WALKING FOR FREEDOM   29

5. THE STRUGGLE GOES ON   38

TIME LINE   44

A TOUR OF THE PAST   45

FURTHER READING   46

WEB SITES   47

SELECT BIBLIOGRAPHY   47

INDEX   48

INTRODUCTION

All her life, Rosa Parks had watched white people tell black people what to do. **She found small ways to stand up for herself and fight for her rights.** But nothing seemed to change.

Then, in Montgomery, Alabama, on December 1, 1955, Rosa **made history**. That day, a bus driver told her to give up her seat to a white person. Black people risked being beaten up or sent to jail if they did not obey the rules. But Rosa was tired of being pushed around. She said no. Her bravery **inspired many other African Americans to** stand up for themselves, too.

This is her story.

....

She found small ways to stand up for herself and fight for her rights. She did not let white people treat her badly or take away her freedoms.

made history did something that changed history

inspired many other African Americans to made many other African Americans want to

When Rosa is growing up in the South, black people are not treated the same as white people. Rosa is angry about how black people are treated. She wants to fight back.

A Hard Childhood

Rosa McCauley was born on February 4, 1913, in Tuskegee, Alabama. When she was two years old, she moved to her grandparents' farm in Pine Level, Alabama. Rosa lived there with her mother, Leona, and her younger brother, Sylvester.

Rosa helped her family by working on their small farm. There were chickens to feed, cows to milk, and a garden to weed. She was a small, shy girl. She obeyed and respected her mother and grandparents. They taught her to **hold her head high** and have dignity.

To earn extra money, Rosa picked cotton on a nearby farm owned by a white farmer. Picking cotton was hard, hot work. But the farmer paid Rosa just fifty cents for a whole day. In some ways, **it didn't seem much different than slavery**.

In the early 1900s, many African American children spent long days working in cotton fields.

---

hold her head high have pride

it didn't seem much different than slavery the farmer still treated the workers like slaves

7

Rosa knew that many black people had worked in the cotton fields of the South during slavery. Her grandparents had told her terrible stories about **their harsh lives as slaves. Slavery had been outlawed** after the Civil War ended in 1865. But many white people still treated African Americans unfairly and cruelly. They were angered by the freedom that black people had gained.

A group of white men called the Ku Klux Klan tried to scare black people. They wanted to stop African Americans from standing up for themselves.

GRANDFATHER SETS AN EXAMPLE

Rosa grew up knowing that most white people believed they were better than black people. Black people were **expected** to call white men and women "Mister" or "Miss." They were not supposed to touch white people or shake hands with them. But Rosa saw her grandfather ignore these rules. When Grandfather met a white man, he treated the man like an equal.

----

their harsh lives as slaves how difficult their lives were when they were slaves

Slavery had been outlawed There were laws that ended slavery

expected supposed

The Ku Klux Klan often carried burning crosses during nighttime rides and parades.

Members of the Ku Klux Klan rode through Southern towns at night wearing white robes and hoods. They burned African American churches and homes. They attacked black people. Sometimes they even killed them.

Some nights they rode right past Rosa's house. Then Grandfather **stayed up and kept watch**. His shotgun **rested** nearby. Rosa **stood guard** with him. Grandfather refused to let any white person take away his dignity. He wasn't afraid. Rosa tried not to be afraid either.

---

stayed up and kept watch stayed awake to protect his family

rested was

stood guard stayed awake

BEFORE YOU MOVE ON...

1. **Author's Point of View** Reread page 7. What does the author think about picking cotton? How do you know?

2. **Inference** Rosa helped her grandfather guard the house. What does this show about her?

LOOK AHEAD Read pages 10–14 to find out why Rosa fights with a white boy.

9

Rosa went to school in a one-room schoolhouse like this one in Georgia.

When Rosa was old enough, she started going to the local school for black children. There was no money for a bus, so everyone walked to and from school. Each day, more than fifty students crowded inside the one-room schoolhouse.

White children went to a **separate** school. They rode on a bus to a new brick building. Often the bus passed the black children as they walked. The white students called the black children **names** and threw garbage out the window. Rosa had been taught not to shout back. That way she wouldn't get into any trouble.

....

separate different
names bad words

Sometimes Rosa just couldn't **keep her anger inside**. When she was about ten years old, she got into a fight with a white boy. Rosa was so mad, she picked up a brick. She told the boy to hit her if he **dared**. After that, the boy left her alone.

Later Rosa told her grandmother what she had done. Instead of being proud of Rosa, Grandmother **scolded** her. Black people should never fight back against white people, Grandmother said. They might get hurt or killed. Grandmother's words confused Rosa. Was she supposed to let another person take away her dignity?

Schools for white children were usually much nicer than schools for black children.

---

keep her anger inside hide her anger

dared was foolish enough

scolded was angry at

Segregation was everywhere in the South. This Coca Cola machine was for white citizens only.

When Rosa was eleven, she went to an African American school for girls in Montgomery. In that city, Rosa **faced** many kinds of segregation for the first time. Segregation meant that black and white people had to be separate. Everywhere Rosa went, she saw **"white only" signs**. Black people couldn't rent a room in a hotel. They couldn't eat inside most restaurants. They had to drink from drinking fountains marked **"colored."** Rosa wondered if the "white" water tasted better.

....

faced saw

"white only" signs signs that said that only white people could enter a place or use something

"colored" black

When she was sixteen, Rosa had to quit school and return home. Her grandmother was sick and needed someone to care for her. Then her mother became ill. Rosa took care of her, too.

Two years later, Rosa met a man named Raymond Parks. What Rosa liked most about Raymond was the way he stood up for himself—and for others. He had been fighting for the rights of black people in Alabama for a long time. In December 1932, Rosa married Raymond and became Mrs. Rosa Parks.

Many restaurants in the South had separate entrances for white and black people.

After her marriage, Rosa decided she wanted to go back to school. Raymond **encouraged her to follow her dream**. In 1933, she finally got her high school diploma.

Even with a high school education, Rosa had a hard time finding a good job. Many white business owners would not **hire** black people. Those who did hire African Americans did not pay them **fair wages**. Rosa found work as a helper in a hospital. At night she sewed for people to make extra money. She hoped that someday life would improve for her and all African Americans.

....

encouraged her to follow her dream wanted her to do what she really wanted to do

hire give jobs to

fair wages enough money

BEFORE YOU MOVE ON...

1. **Cause and Effect** Rosa fought because the boy was going to hit her. Why did Rosa's grandmother scold her?

2. **Inference** Reread page 12. How do you think segregation made black and white people feel?

LOOK AHEAD Read pages 15–21 to see why Rosa refuses to take the elevator.

Rosa does little things to fight the unfair rules.
She thinks segregation on buses is especially unfair.

2 UNFAIR RULES

Rosa hated all the different ways that black people were **mistreated**. She especially hated segregation. At first, she found quiet ways to **fight back**.

....

mistreated treated badly

fight back show she did not agree with segregation

Instead of taking the "colored" elevator, she walked up the stairs. She wouldn't use the "colored" drinking fountain, either. Even if she was thirsty, Rosa waited until she got home to have a glass of water.

Rosa especially disliked the segregation on the city buses. Most of the people who rode the buses were African American. They paid the same amount of money as white people did. But they were not treated the same.

A Montgomery bus

Signs on segregated buses told black people were they could and could not sit.

Black riders **stepped on** the bus in front to pay **their ten-cent fare**. Then they had to get off and enter again through the back door. Sometimes a driver would **zoom off** before a person got on again.

Inside the bus, black people had to sit in the back rows. The front seats were for white people only. African Americans could sit in the middle rows if no white people wanted the seats. But if a white person wanted to sit down, all the black people in that row of seats had to stand. **A black person was not allowed to** sit in the same row as a white person.

....

stepped on entered

their ten-cent fare ten cents for the ride

zoom off quickly drive away

A black person was not allowed to There was a law that said black people could not

Rosa walked whenever she could. But she had to take the bus to get to her job. Riding a segregated bus made her mad. Once she **refused to** enter in the back after paying her fare. The bus driver grabbed her by the sleeve and made her **get off**.

Rosa wanted to help make life better for black people. She knew she couldn't do it by herself. In December of 1943, she joined the National Association for the Advancement of Colored People, the NAACP.

The NAACP had offices in cities across the United States.

---

refused to would not

get off leave the bus

Rosa used her sewing skills to get by. But her real work was fighting for civil rights.

The NAACP **worked for the civil rights of African Americans everywhere**. Civil rights are the rights of all citizens to enjoy life, freedom, and equal rights.

Rosa agreed to be the secretary for the NAACP in Montgomery. She spent all day at her job sewing at the Montgomery Fair department store. Then she went to the NAACP office to **volunteer** there.

As the NAACP secretary, Rosa wrote letters and answered the phones. She traveled from town to town in Alabama meeting with African Americans.

---

worked for the civil rights of African Americans everywhere wanted to change laws that tell what an African American can and cannot do in America

volunteer do work without being paid

Rosa talked to other black people about the **unjust** ways they were treated. She tried to get them to **register to vote**. That way, they could **elect** better leaders. But there were many unfair rules that kept African Americans from voting. It took Rosa three years to get past all those rules and vote for the first time.

THE TEST

To vote, white and black people in Alabama had to pass a test. They had to prove they could read, write, and understand the laws of the United States. The people who gave the test made it almost impossible for African Americans to pass. Rosa had to take the test three times. Each time, she believed she had passed. But the state wouldn't let her vote until **her third try**. Then she had to pay a tax. The tax was much higher for black people than for most white people. It cost Rosa almost half a week's wages to be able to vote.

....

unjust unfair
register to vote sign a paper so they could vote
elect choose
her third try the third time she took the test

20

In 1954, Rosa heard some good news. The nation's highest court, the Supreme Court, said that schools could not be segregated. It said that black and white students had to **learn** together. The Court's decision made many white people in the South angry. They tried to **fight** it. But Rosa and other African Americans knew that **times were** finally beginning to change.

....

learn go to school
fight stop
times were life was

BEFORE YOU MOVE ON...

1. **Inference** Rosa would not use anything that was just for "colored" people. Why?

2. **Conclusions** Reread "The Test" on page 20. Why did many African Americans not vote in elections?

LOOK AHEAD Read pages 22–28 to find out what happens when Rosa refuses to give her bus seat to a white man.

When a white man wants Rosa's bus seat, she quietly says no. The police arrest her. African Americans hear the news and decide to stop riding the buses.

3 ROSA SAYS NO

Thursday, December 1, 1955, started as a normal day for Rosa Parks. She worked at the Montgomery Fair department store until five at night. Then she **boarded** the Cleveland Avenue bus to go home.

---

boarded got on

Rosa paid her fare and got on in the back of the bus. She noticed that the driver was the one who had **thrown her off** the bus years earlier. Usually Rosa would wait for another bus when she saw this driver. But this time, Rosa stayed on the bus. She just wanted to get home.

Rosa found a seat in the middle section. During the ride, a white man boarded the bus. There were no more seats in the **white section**. So the driver told Rosa and the others in her row to move to the back.

Bus drivers were expected to keep their buses segregated.

....

thrown her off told her to leave
white section part of the bus where only white people sat

**Rosa Parks
in the 1950s**

The other African Americans stood up. Rosa didn't **budge**. She just moved closer to the window. She was tired. But she wasn't tired from working. She was tired of being mistreated.

The bus driver asked her if she was going to move. "No. I am not," she answered. Then he said he was going to **have the police** arrest her. "You may do that," Rosa said quietly. She wasn't afraid. She thought about her grandfather, and she felt strong.

---

budge stand
have the police tell the police to

Two police officers arrived. One asked Rosa why she didn't move. Instead of answering, she asked him a question: "Why do **you all push us around**?" The police officer said, "I don't know, but **the law is the law** and you're under arrest."

In jail, Rosa felt very much alone. Still, she held her head high. She knew she was doing the right thing. Later, she called her mother and Raymond. Raymond hurried to the police station and paid a fee so that he could take her home.

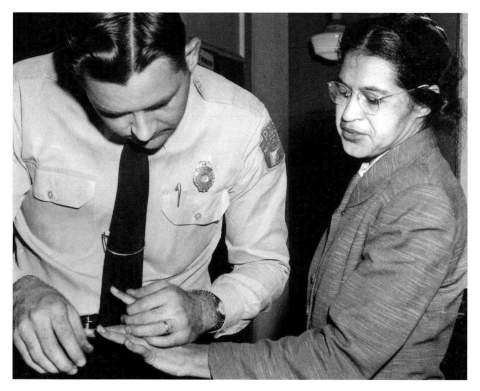

A police officer takes Rosa's fingerprints.

....

you all push us around white people tell black people what to do
the law is the law the law cannot be questioned

That night, an African American leader named E. D. Nixon came to see Rosa. He had heard about her arrest. He wanted to **take her case to court**. It might be a way to prove that segregation on the buses was unfair and should be against the law. **Was Rosa willing?**

Raymond **pleaded with** Rosa not to go to court. He thought white people might try to kill her if she fought against her arrest. But Rosa was tired of **giving in to** white people. After some thought, she agreed to go to court.

E. D. Nixon became an important leader in the fight for civil rights.

---

take her case to court ask a judge to decide if Rosa did something wrong

Was Rosa willing? Would Rosa go to court?

pleaded with begged

giving in to being afraid of

"They've Messed with the Wrong One"

Rosa was not the first African American to be arrested on a segregated bus. In the spring of 1955, a teenager named Claudette Colvin had fought to keep her seat. That summer, a girl named Mary Louise Smith did the same thing. Rosa Parks **stood out** because she was a grown woman. People respected her. When one woman saw Rosa, she said, "They've messed with the wrong one now."

E. D. Nixon was not the only person who had heard about Rosa's arrest. **The news had spread throughout the city.** It made many black people angry. Rosa Parks was a good woman, they said. How could the police arrest her?

The next night Rosa met with about fifty African American ministers and other community leaders. They came up with a plan to fight against segregation on the buses.

....

stood out was noticed

The news had spread throughout the city. Many people in the city heard the news.

The ministers would tell people in their churches to boycott the buses, or refuse to ride them, for one day. They would ask black cab drivers to stop at bus stops and pick up passengers for only ten cents, the same price as a bus ride. Many other people would have to walk to work.

Anyone who boycotted the buses **would be taking a big risk**. They might be **harmed** by angry white people. In the past, most African Americans had been afraid to take that kind of risk. Rosa and the other black leaders wondered if the black people of Montgomery would **walk for freedom** now.

....

would be taking a big risk could be in danger

harmed hurt

walk for freedom stop taking the bus to show they wanted fair treatment

BEFORE YOU MOVE ON...

1. **Sequence** Rosa was arrested. Tell what happened on December 1, 1955, after Rosa left work.

2. **Cause and Effect** What effect did Rosa's arrest have on black people?

LOOK AHEAD Read pages 29–33 to find out what happens in court.

Rosa is not alone. Many others join in the fight to end segregation. African Americans in Montgomery stop riding buses. Finally one segregation law is changed.

WHY FIGHT TRAFFI
GO BY BUS

4 WALKING FOR FREEDOM

Monday, December 5, was a big day. It was the day of the boycott. It was also Rosa's **day in court**.

---

day in court day to go to court

Rosa stands trial for refusing to obey bus segregation.

Rosa's **trial** lasted for only five minutes. The judge said that Rosa had broken the law. He ordered her to pay $14. Rosa's lawyers were not ready to **give up**. They wanted to take the **case** of bus segregation all the way to the Supreme Court.

Rosa lost her case, but she had stood up for her rights with dignity. Thousands of African Americans followed her example that day. Instead of riding the bus, they walked to work. Some rode in cabs with black drivers. Others **carpooled**. The buses were nearly empty.

....

trial time with a judge in court

give up quit

case problem

carpooled rode in cars with several people

To everyone's surprise, the day-long boycott had been a success. The African Americans of Montgomery had sent a strong message to the city. They were not going to be pushed around anymore.

That night, Rosa **attended** another meeting. This time, nearly five thousand people **showed up**. They couldn't all **fit** inside, so some stood outside. When Rosa got there, she squeezed through the crowd. She was given a seat in front.

Boycotters in Montgomery often met at the Dexter Avenue Baptist Church.

....

attended went to
showed up came
fit find a place

The **purpose of** the meeting was to decide whether to continue the boycott. A young black minister named Martin Luther King, Jr., got up to speak. **His powerful voice filled the room.**

It was time for the black people of Montgomery to **come together**, he said. It was time for them to stand up for their rights. People liked what he had to say. They agreed that the boycott should go on. So did Rosa.

Martin Luther King, Jr., inspired the boycotters to keep up their protest against segregation.

....

purpose of reason for

His powerful voice filled the room. He had a strong voice.

come together work with each other

A GREAT LEADER

Martin Luther King, Jr., inspired many people in the 1950s and 1960s. He led what became known as the civil rights movement. King taught African Americans to **demand their rights** without using violence. He led peaceful protests such as boycotts and marches. He also gave powerful speeches. King said that all people deserved to be free from hatred and unfair treatment. His ideas and words helped African Americans win their rights.

After Martin's speech, someone asked Rosa to stand. Shyly, Rosa got up from her seat and looked at the crowd in front of her. Right away, everyone else in the room **shot up to their feet** and began clapping. "Thank you, sister," they shouted through the applause. Rosa Parks had become **a hero**.

---

demand their rights tell others what they wanted

shot up to their feet quickly stood

a hero someone they admired

BEFORE YOU MOVE ON...

1. **Cause and Effect** Rosa set an example. How did African Americans follow her example?

2. **Comparisons** Reread page 33. How were Martin Luther King, Jr., and Rosa Parks alike and different?

LOOK AHEAD Read pages 34–37 to find out why the boycott was so difficult for African Americans.

Downtown Montgomery was a busy shopping area before the bus boycott.

The boycott did go on, week after week and month after month. It made big news in cities and countries around the world. People began sending money to civil rights leaders in Montgomery. They wanted to help keep the boycott going.

Many white people in Montgomery wanted to **put a stop to** the boycott. It was **giving the city a bad reputation**. The bus company was losing a lot of money. And downtown business owners had lost many customers. Black people weren't taking the buses to their shops anymore.

....

put a stop to end

giving the city a bad reputation making the city look like a bad place

Police began to **badger** African Americans waiting for cabs. They told the cab drivers they would be arrested for **not charging full fare**. They even put some black leaders in jail. Still, African Americans refused to ride the buses.

In the midst of it all, Rosa lost her job. Many people lost their jobs because of their work on the boycott. Some people said this was what had happened to Rosa. Rosa wasn't worried. She earned money by sewing at home instead.

Rosa became a spokesperson for the boycotters of Montgomery.

....

badger cause trouble for

not charging full fare letting African Americans pay only ten cents

In the midst of it all During this time

Rosa walks up the steps to court with E. D. Nixon for another trial on bus segregation in Montgomery.

What upset Rosa much more than losing her job were the angry phone calls and letters she got. Some white people thought Rosa **was to blame for** the boycott. They **threatened to** hurt her and her family.

Other black leaders were also threatened. One night, someone threw a bomb at Martin Luther King's house. The houses of other African American leaders were bombed, too. Bombs also **blew up** in the homes of white people who helped with the boycott. Still, the boycott continued.

....

was to blame for caused
threatened to said they would
blew up exploded

The buses of Montgomery stayed empty for more than a year. But the city leaders refused to end segregation on the buses. Finally, the Supreme Court decided that segregation on buses was against the law. It said that bus drivers in Montgomery had to let African Americans sit anywhere they wanted.

Martin Luther King called everyone together and told them the good news. On December 21, 1956, after 381 days, the boycott ended. It was an important **victory**. But Rosa knew that African Americans had many more **battles to fight**.

....

victory success
battles to fight things to try to change

BEFORE YOU MOVE ON...

1. **Opinion** The bus boycott caused African Americans many hardships. Was it worth it?
2. **Theme** How does the bus boycott relate to the theme Pulling Together?

LOOK AHEAD Read pages 38–43 to find out what Rosa did after the boycott ended.

Rosa continues to fight for change. Now many people work together for civil rights. They start to see some success when new, fair laws are passed.

5 THE STRUGGLE GOES ON

Rosa's life **did not go back to** normal after the boycott ended. People still threatened her and her family. No one wanted to hire her. Finally, in 1957, Rosa decided to leave Montgomery with her mother and Raymond.

....

did not go back to was not

The family moved to Detroit, Michigan. Rosa's brother, Sylvester, lived there. Raymond got a job at a barber school. Rosa worked at a clothing factory.

Rosa was no longer **in the spotlight**. But she still fought to change segregation and unfair treatment of African Americans. Her bravery and the bravery of the Montgomery boycotters had inspired people throughout the country. Many other African Americans began working for civil rights in cities across the South.

Rosa sits near the front of a Montgomery bus after bus segregation has ended.

---

in the spotlight being given a lot of attention

In the summer of 1963, Rosa went to Washington, D.C., for a protest called the March on Washington. More than 250,000 people **gathered in the nation's capital** to support civil rights for African Americans. Many people, including Martin Luther King, Jr., **gave speeches**. The March on Washington let the U.S. government know that black people were serious about their freedom.

The March on Washington was the biggest civil rights march in history.

---

gathered in the nation's capital went to Washington, D.C.

gave speeches spoke to everyone there

Rosa continued to speak out for the rights of black people in the United States and around the world.

Finally, in 1964, President Lyndon Johnson signed the Civil Rights Act. This new law said that African Americans had to be treated fairly and equally. It ended segregation in all public places, such as parks, hotels, and restaurants. It also said that black people had to be treated fairly in their jobs.

In 1965, the president signed another law called the Voting Rights Act. It said that states could not stop African Americans from voting. Rosa knew that the two laws did not solve all the problems. But they **created** important changes for African Americans.

....

created were

That same year, an important change happened in Rosa's life. For the first time, she found a job that she loved. She went to work for an African American **congressman** named John Conyers. She answered phones, met with visitors, and **kept track of** the congressman's schedule. Conyers also asked Rosa to help him improve the lives of black people in Michigan. Part of Rosa's job was to find **housing for the homeless**. She worked for Congressman Conyers for twenty-three years.

ROSA TELLS HER STORY

Many years had passed since Rosa refused to give up her seat on the bus. But she was still famous. People wanted to learn about her. In the 1990s, she published three books about her life. She called them *Rosa Parks: My Story; Quiet Strength;* and *I Am Rosa Parks.* Rosa's fourth book, *Dear Mrs. Parks,* is a collection of letters she has received from children.

congressman politician
kept track of organized
housing for the homeless places to live for people
without homes

Rosa has won many medals for her bravery and leadership.

Rosa had seen many changes happen in her lifetime. She had learned many lessons about facing problems with courage. She wanted to share what she had learned with young African Americans. In 1987, she helped open the Rosa and Raymond Parks Institute for Self Development. The institute teaches young African Americans about black history. It also teaches them to have dignity, pride, and self-respect.

Rosa Parks still inspires people to stand up for themselves. Her bravery will be remembered for **a long time to come**.

....

a long time to come many years

BEFORE YOU MOVE ON...

1. **Conclusions** Why do you think Rosa's life was not the same after the boycott?
2. **Inference** Reread page 42. Why do you think Rosa's job with the congressman was the first job she loved?

LOOK AHEAD Read pages 44–47 to find more information about Rosa and segregation.

TIME LINE

In the year ...

1915 Rosa moved to Pine Level with her mother and younger brother. | Age 2 |

1924 she moved to Montgomery to go to school.

1932 she married Raymond Parks in December.

1943 she joined the NAACP. | Age 30 |

1946 she voted for the first time.

1954 the Supreme Court ruled that schools could not be segregated.

1955 she was arrested for refusing to give up her seat on the bus on December 1. | Age 42 |
she went to court and was found guilty of breaking the law on December 5.
the Montgomery bus boycott began on December 5.

1956 the Supreme Court ruled that buses in Montgomery could not be segregated.

1957 she and her family moved to Detroit.

1963 she went to the March on Washington in Washington, D.C. | Age 50 |

1964 President Lyndon Johnson signed the Civil Rights Act of 1964.

1965 President Johnson signed the Voting Rights Act of 1965.
she began working for Congressman John Conyers of Michigan.

1977 Raymond Parks died.

1987 she helped open the Rosa and Raymond Parks Institute for Self Development. | Age 74 |

2000 The Troy State University Montgomery Rosa Parks Library and Museum opened on December 1.

A TOUR OF THE PAST

Imagine that you could go back in time to see Rosa Parks's famous arrest, or go to the bus boycott meeting, or to meet Martin Luther King, Jr. At one museum in Montgomery, Alabama, you can.

The Troy State University Montgomery Rosa Parks Library and Museum opened in 2000. It **honors** Rosa Parks and civil rights in Montgomery. The museum has a **life-size model of** the bus Rosa rode in on December 1, 1955. Through the windows, you can see a film in which actors **portray** Rosa's famous arrest. In another room, you can experience the large meetings held during the Montgomery bus boycott. You can even visit a reproduction of Martin Luther King, Jr., in his home. Near the end of the tour, visitors can sit down in a back row of bus seats. Imagine being on the bus with Rosa that famous day. What would you have done?

----

honors remembers
life-size model of bus that is the same size as
portray show

BEFORE YOU MOVE ON...

1. **Viewing** How does the timeline on page 44 help you understand the book better?

2. **Author's Purpose** Reread page 45. Why do you think the author chose to include information about this museum?

45

FURTHER READING

NONFICTION

Isaacs, Sally Senzell. *America in the Time of Martin Luther King, Jr.: 1948 to 1976.* **Chicago, IL: Heinemann Library, 2000.** Describes events in our nation during the time of the civil rights movement and beyond.

King, Casey, and Linda Barrett Osborne. *Oh Freedom! Kids Talk about the Civil Rights Movement with the People Who Made It Happen.* **New York: Random House, 1997.** Children interview activists and ordinary citizens about their experiences during the civil rights era.

Welch, Catherine A. *Children of the Civil Rights Era.* **Minneapolis: Carolrhoda Books, Inc. 2001.** Tells the story of the civil rights movement from the point of view of children and young adults who experienced it.

Winget, Mary. *Martin Luther King Jr.* **Minneapolis: Lerner Publications Company, 2003.** A biography of this important civil rights leader from his childhood to his death.

FICTION

Curtis, Christopher Paul. *The Watsons Go to Birmingham—1963.* **New York: Delacorte Press, 1995.** In this novel the Watson family travels from their home in Flint, Michigan, to Birmingham, Alabama, to visit relatives.

Gray, Libba Moore. *Dear Willie Rudd.* **New York: Simon & Schuster, 1993.** A woman remembers the African American housekeeper who helped raise her, and thinks about how life could have been fairer for Willie.

Miller, William. *The Bus Ride.* **New York: Lee & Low Books, 1998.** With an introduction by Rosa Parks, this story is about a fictional girl named Sara who doesn't understand why she and her mother must sit at the back of the bus.

WEB SITES

Girl Power! Spotlight on Rosa Parks
<www.girlpower.gov/girlarea/gpguests/RosaParks.htm>
Geared for young people, this website includes information about Mrs. Parks, a reading list, and helpful links.

Rosa and Raymond Parks Institute for Self Development
<www.rosaparksinstitute.org> The official website of Rosa Parks's organization dedicated to African American youth.

Rosa Parks: Civil Rights Pioneer
<www.achievement.org/autodoc/page/par0int-1> A 1995 interview with Mrs. Parks about her life and her role in the civil rights movement.

The Troy State University Montgomery Rosa Parks Library and Museum
<www.tsum.edu/museum> Information about this museum dedicated to Rosa Parks, with links to other related websites.

SELECT BIBLIOGRAPHY

Brinkley, Douglas. *Rosa Parks.* New York: Viking Penguin, 2000.

Parks, Rosa, with Gregory J. Reed. *Dear Mrs. Parks: A Dialogue with Today's Youth.* New York: Lee & Low, 1996.

Parks, Rosa, with Gregory J. Reed. *Quiet Strength: The Faith, the Hope, and the Heart of a Woman Who Changed A Nation.* Grand Rapids, MI: Zondervan Publishing, 1994.

Parks, Rosa, with Jim Haskins. *Rosa Parks: My Story.* New York: Dial Books, 1992.

INDEX

Arrest, 23–25

Birth, 6
Books by Rosa Parks, 42
Boycott of buses, 28–31, 34–37
Buses, 16–18

Childhood, 6–12
Civil rights, 19, 39, 40
Civil Rights Act of 1964, 41
Colvin, Claudette, 27
Conyers, John, 42

Detroit, Michigan, 39
Dexter Avenue Baptist Church, 31

Grandfather, 7, 8, 9
Grandmother, 7, 8, 11, 13

Jobs, 14
Johnson, President Lyndon, 41

King, Martin Luther, Jr., 32–33, 36, 37
Ku Klux Klan, 8–9

March on Washington, 40
McCauley, Leona, 6, 7, 13, 39
McCauley, Sylvester, 6, 39

Montgomery, Alabama, 12
Montgomery Fair department store, 19, 22

NAACP (National Association for the Advancement of Colored People), 18–20
Nixon, E. D., 26, 36

Parks, Raymond, 13–14, 25, 26, 39
Pine Level, Alabama, 6

Rosa and Raymond Parks Institute for Self Development, 43
Rosa Parks Library and Museum, 45

Schools in the South, 10, 11, 21
Segregation, 10, 12, 15–17, 39
Slavery, 7–8
Smith, Mary Louise, 27
Supreme Court, 21, 37

Threats, 36
Trial, 29–30
Tuskegee, Alabama, 6

Voting, 20
Voting Rights Act of 1965, 41

Acknowledgments

For photographs: AP/Wide World Photos: p25, p26, p30, p31, p34, p36;
Birmingham Public Library: p17 (Department of Archives and Manuscripts (49.59), Birmingham, AL); **Brown Brothers:** p9, p32; **CORBIS:** p35 (© Bettmann), p41 (© Bettmann); **Getty Images:** p7 (© Sheldon Hine/Hulton Archive Photos), p40 (© Hulton Archive Photos); **Hulton Archive Photos:** p23 (© Tony Vaccaro); **Independent Picture Service:** p19 (Todd Strand); **Library of Congress:** p10 (LC-USF34-046235-D), p11 (LC-USF34-031305-D), p12 (LC-USZ62-116815), p13 (LC-USF33-20513-M2), p18 (LC-USZ62-33783), p39 (LC-USZ62-111235); **Schomburg Center for Research in Black Culture, The New York Public Library:** front and back covers, p4, p16, p24, p43

For quoted material: p. 24, Rosa Parks, *Quiet Strength* (Grand Rapids, MI: Zondervan Publishing, 1994.); pp. 24, 25, 27, Rosa Parks, *Rosa Parks: My Story* (New York; Dial Books, 1992.); p. 33, Douglas Brinkley, *Rosa Parks* (New York: Viking Penguin, 2000).